For the Duration

For the Duration

♡ dePAOLA

written and illustrated by

Tomie dePaola

A 26 FAIRMOUNT AVENUE BOOK

G. P. Putnam's Sons • Penguin Young Readers Group

G. P. PUTNAM'S SONS A division of Penguin Young Readers Group. Published by The Penguin Group. Penguin Group (USA) Inc., 375 Hudson Street, New York, NY 10014, U.S.A. Penguin Group (Canada), 90 Eglinton Avenue East, Suite 700, Toronto, Ontario M4P 2Y3, Canada (a division of Pearson Penguin Canada Inc.). Penguin Books Ltd, 80 Strand, London WC2R 0RL, England. Penguin Ireland, 25 St. Stephen's Green, Dublin 2, Ireland (a division of Penguin Books Ltd.). Penguin Group (Australia), 250 Camberwell Road, Camberwell, Victoria 3124, Australia (a division of Pearson Australia Group Pty Ltd). Penguin Books India Pvt Ltd, 11 Community Centre, Panchsheel Park, New Delhi - 110 017, India. Penguin Group (NZ), 67 Apollo Drive, Rosedale, North Shore 0632, New Zealand (a division of Pearson New Zealand Ltd). Penguin Books (South Africa) (Pty) Ltd, 24 Sturdee Avenue, Rosebank, Johannesburg 2196, South Africa. Penguin Books Ltd, Registered Offices: 80 Strand, London WC2R 0RL, England.

Published simultaneously in Canada. Printed in the United States of America. Book design by Marikka Tamura. Text set in Garth Graphic. Library of Congress Cataloging-in-Publication Data De Paola, Tomie. For the duration : the war years / written and illustrated by Tomie dePaola. p. cm. — (A 26 Fairmount Avenue book ; 8) 1. De Paola, Tomie—Childhood and youth—Juvenile literature. 2. De Paola, Tomie—Homes and haunts—Connecticut—Meriden—Juvenile literature. 3. Authors, American—20th century—Biography—Juvenile literature. 4. Illustrators—United States—Biography—Juvenile literature. 5. World War, 1939–1945—Connecticut—Juvenile literature. I. Title.   PS3554.E11474Z474 2009 813'.54—dc22 [B] 2008026733

ISBN 978-0-399-25209-9

1 3 5 7 9 10 8 6 4 2

*For all the people in Meriden, Connecticut,
who worked hard "for the duration"*

Chapter One

Friday, May 1, 1942

Dear Diary,
   Today, a sad thing happened to me at school. I ran out of the music room crying because my cousin Blackie was killed in the war.
              Y. B. F. I. T. W.
                   TOMIE

This afternoon, Mr. Conklin, the music supervisor, came to King Street School. It was going to be the first rehearsal for our Special Choir, which will sing at the Memorial Day assembly at the end of the month.

Memorial Day is also called Decoration Day. It is the day when people decorate the

1

graves of the men and women who fought in all the wars, with flowers and small American flags.

All the kids bring cut flowers from our moms' and dads' gardens to school the morning before Memorial Day. At King Street, Mr. Walters, the janitor, always puts pots and containers filled with water in the front hallway of the school. The kids put the bunches of flowers in the pots and later on some workers come in a truck to gather them all up and take them to the cemeteries around town. This year we'll bring the flowers to school on Friday because Memorial Day is on Saturday.

Mr. Conklin chose twenty students for the Special Choir, four from each class, starting with the second grade. He chose the ones whose voices he liked the best from the music classes we had had all year.

I was picked from our class with my best friend, Jeannie Houdlette. A girl named Sylvia was picked from the other second grade (she has a beautiful soprano voice) along with another boy who I didn't know too well. We all met in the music room upstairs on the second floor of the old part of the school.

You could tell where the old part was because the wooden floors squeaked more than in the new part.

Miss Mulligan, the fifth-grade teacher, came into the music room with a pile of music sheets in her arms. One of the older students passed them out. Miss Mulligan played the piano at all our assemblies.

"Now, girls and boys," Mr. Conklin said, "we will sing a *medley*, which is what we call a collection of songs that are sung one

after the other. Our medley will be four songs that represent the four branches of the service: the Army, the Navy, the Marines, and the Army Air Corps.

"And," Mr. Conklin added, "we will sing in PARTS!"

Miss Mulligan called out our names and told us which section we would be in. I had a nice high voice, so I was in the soprano section. Two third-grade boys were in the soprano section, too. Jeannie was an alto. She could sing a little lower than me. And she could read music because she was learning to play the piano. I didn't really know how to read music, but I was told I had a "good ear" because after hearing a melody just once, I could remember it. And I had what Mr. Conklin called "perfect pitch."

Miss Mulligan sat down
at the piano and played
the first song in the
medley. It was the
U.S. Army anthem.
The beginning words
were:

"Over hill, over dale,
We have hit the
dusty trail
And the Caissons
go rolling along."
(A caisson is a
wagon that carries
ammunition.)

"Very good," Mr. Conklin said. "Now
we'll try the second song in the medley,
which is 'Anchors Aweigh,' the U.S. Navy
anthem."

We sang:
"Anchors Aweigh, my boys,
Anchors Aweigh.
Farewell to college joys,
We sail at break of day-ay-ay-ay."

"Now, Miss Mulligan will play the alto parts for both songs," Mr. Conklin told us.

The altos practiced, then the tenors and basses, who were all the older boys whose voices had changed—or who could at least sing lower.

We went on to practice "The Marines' Hymn."

"From the Halls of Montezuma
To the shores of Tripoli,
We fight our country's battles
In the air, on land, and sea."

"We will now practice the last song in the medley, learn the parts, and try to put them all together," Mr. Conklin said. "It is the Army Air Corps anthem."

Miss Mulligan began and we sang:
"Off we go into the wide blue yonder."

I started to feel funny. I started to think of my cousin Blackie, whose plane was shot down. I couldn't help it. I started imagining the enemy planes shooting at Blackie's bomber.

All of a sudden the words went: "We live in fame or go down in flame."

Blackie went down in flames, I thought, *down in flames.*

Tears welled up in my eyes and my throat began to choke and it was hard to breathe. I jumped up. I couldn't help it. I ran out of the music room, down the hall, to the second floor boys' room. I fell against the wall and started to sob and sob and sob.

Suddenly, Mr. Conklin came in.

"Tommy," he said, "whatever is the matter?"

I could hardly talk, I was crying so hard. Mr. Conklin lifted me up and took me out into the hallway. Miss Mulligan took me by the shoulders into the teachers' room. The doors to the classrooms were open and kids looked out at me.

When we got inside the teachers' room, Miss Mulligan asked me very quietly, "Can you tell me what's wrong, Tommy?"

"My cousin Blackie was killed when his plane was shot down. The Air Corps song made me think about it and I couldn't stop," I sobbed.

"Here," Miss Mulligan said, handing me some tissues. "Wipe your nose and try to dry your eyes. I'm going to take you down to the nurse's office, where you can lie down."

We went down the stairs to Miss Luby's office. I lay down on the little cot that was against the wall. Miss Mulligan gave me a

paper cup of water and pulled down the window shade so the room wasn't bright anymore.

"You rest and I'll be back in a minute," said Miss Mulligan. She went out the door and closed it.

As much as I tried, I just couldn't stop my tears from coming. My stomach hurt. I couldn't catch my breath. I just wanted to go home.

The door to the room opened and there were Miss Mulligan, Miss Burke, the principal, Miss Gardner, my teacher, and my brother, Buddy. Miss Gardner had my jacket.

"Tommy," Miss Burke said, "Joseph will take you home. We called your mother and she's waiting for you. Now, put on your jacket and we'll see you on Monday."

Buddy and I left even though school wasn't over yet.

Buddy looked mad. "Hurry up!" he yelled. He walked fast and ahead of me.

I had to run to keep up.

"Thanks a lot," Buddy said. "My friends are going to laugh at me because of you."

I didn't say anything. I didn't know what was wrong.

• • •

When we got home, Mom was waiting at the door. She hugged me.

"You go right upstairs to the bathroom, Tomie, and wash your face with a cold cloth."

While I was in the bathroom, I heard Buddy talking to Mom. "I'm so glad that I go to Lincoln Junior High School next year and won't *ever* have to be in the same school as him as long as I live!"

"Buddy, watch your tone," Mom scolded.

"I don't care. All my friends are going to laugh at me. It's all over the school: Tomie dePaola ran out of the music room, crying like a BABY!"

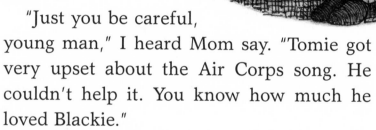

"Just you be careful, young man," I heard Mom say. "Tomie got very upset about the Air Corps song. He couldn't help it. You know how much he loved Blackie."

"He always does stuff so everyone pays attention to him," Buddy answered. "It embarrasses me! He's a big sissy. Everyone thinks so."

"That's enough, Buddy," Mom said. "I think you'd better go up to your room and cool off."

Mom came to the stairs. "Tomie," she called, "come down."

11

Buddy stormed up the stairs.

I was just coming out of the bathroom. As Buddy passed me, he punched me—hard—in the arm.

"I'll get even with you!" he growled.

I ran down the stairs. That night I slept on the daybed in my baby sister Maureen's room. Mom said Buddy needed to "simmer down."

Chapter Two

Saturday, May 2, 1942

Dear Diary,
I'm writing this in Palmer
Method. Mom said to practice
my penmanship and maybe
Miss Gardner will notice that
I'm getting better at it.

Today Mom told me that
Miss Leah has a surprise
for me at Dancing School.

I can't wait to find out
what it is.
Y. B. I. I. T. W.

Tomie

mmmmm drill 13 mmmmm

I love going to Miss Leah's Dancing School every Saturday. The only thing is that it means I can't go down to my grandparents' store in Wallingford to help out Tom and Nana, like Dad and Buddy do. But since we go to Tom and Nana's house every Sunday, I still get to spend time with Tom. Tom is really my best grown-up friend since Dad is working two jobs—his regular job during the day at the State Office Building in Hartford and at night at the New Departure War Plant. Tom is the one I talk to about things that worry me, like the war.

This spring I am allowed to go downtown to Dancing School all by myself on the bus. The South Meriden bus driver on Saturdays is Mr. Al Comeau. Al and Mrs. Comeau are good friends of Mom and Dad and they live just down the street on Baldwin Street. They have a house that is just about the same size as ours. They also have a couple of kids who have their own bedrooms (not like us—Buddy and I have to share). But they go to Hanover School, not King Street, so we don't see them much, except in the summer when all the kids from all the streets in the neighborhood play together. In the Comeaus' house there are two very fancy statues on the mantel of the fireplace. One is a lady wearing a dress and apron holding a big bunch of wheat, and the other is a man in overalls with a big hay rake over his shoulder. They are painted very bright colors, and I bet they cost a lot of money!

To get downtown, I'd walk down Fairmount Avenue to Highland Avenue. Then I'd go up Highland to where it met Columbus Avenue. That was the bus stop. Some of the houses I walked by had flags with a blue star in their windows. The government gave these flags to the mothers if they had a son or daughter fighting in the war. I see more and more of these flags every day. Some houses have two or three flags. Mom told me that Aunt Kate will get a flag with a gold star on it because Cousin Blackie was killed. The gold star means that the mother's son or daughter gave his or her life for the country.

If I was a little late for the bus, and Mr. Al Comeau was driving, he'd wait for me. The bus cost one dime or a token. You could get three tokens for twenty-five cents.

The bus would go down Columbus Avenue, which was a long hill, to Hanover Street to Cook Avenue. Then it went up Cook Avenue (another hill) and turned down West Main Street.

The bus passed the YMCA, then the Palace movie theater where I saw all the Judy Garland and Mickey Rooney musicals. Across from the Palace was Lamphier's Paint and Art Supplies store. I liked going in there to look at all the oil paints, watercolors, pastels, and books on how to draw. There were lots of other stores, too: Katz Brothers Sweet Shoppe, where all the high school kids went after school; Woolworth's Five- and Ten-Cent Store, which always had the best Halloween stuff; Connecticut Light and Power Company, which looked liked the picture of a Greek temple I saw

in a book; Growers Outlet Grocery Store; Christian Fox Music Store, where you could listen to records in little booths before you bought them; Alexander's Candy and Popcorn store, where Mom got me popcorn so I wouldn't be carsick on long trips; and the Vienna Bakery, which always had decorated cakes in the window. There was a traffic tower that stood in the middle of West Main Street and Colony Street; Molloy's Stationery, which sold beautiful fountain pens; a couple of shoe stores; and the Alling Rubber Sports store, where Mrs. Anderson's husband worked. (Mrs. Anderson played the piano at Miss Leah's.)

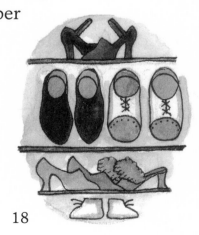

The bus would turn the corner at Schulte's Smoke Shop, and there was the bus depot. The bus ride took thirty minutes.

Today I got off the bus and walked as fast as I could to Miss Leah's to find out what the surprise would be. I crossed the train tracks that went right through the middle of downtown to get to the Hamrah Building. That was one of the biggest brick buildings in all of Meriden. It was very old and a little spooky. Miss Leah's Dancing School was on the top floor. The stairs were very wide and went up and up and up. It had a lot of dark corners and hallways on every floor.

But Miss Leah's Dancing School was bright and shiny, with big mirrors on one wall so we could watch ourselves practicing. There was a room called the "waiting room" where sometimes Miss Leah's mom, Mrs. Grossman, sat at the desk. Mrs. Clarence Anderson was the piano player. Her piano was in the big room with the mirrors. There were ballet bars along the walls, too.

Carol Morrissey, Patty Clark, Billy Burns, and I were the only ones in the advanced class that year, so everything we did was in "partners." Carol and Patty went to King Street School with me. Carol, who was my partner, was in first grade. Patty was in my second-grade class and her partner, Billy, went to a different school.

When we got to class, the first thing we did was to warm up with simple tap steps, like "up-back-down," "slaps," and "time steps." Then we would do our "travel steps," going across the floor one at a time. As we got better, Miss Leah added turns and harder things like that. She taught us to "spot out turns," which meant that we'd look at a spot on the wall, start to turn our bodies, then whip our heads around to look back at the same spot before our bodies got there. If you did it right, you didn't get dizzy.

Then we'd start working on our "routine" —the dance we would do in the recital. Every week, Miss Leah would give us some new steps to add. We would finally do all the steps to the music. I loved it! Mom wrote down all the steps for me in a little notebook so I could practice every night at home.

• • •

This Saturday, when class was over, Billy
Burns and I practiced "Uncle Sam Gets
Around," the special number we would sing
and recite. Then Miss Leah said, "Tomie,
would you please wait a few minutes? I want
to talk with you."

This must be the surprise that Mom told
me about!

"Tomie," Miss Leah said, "my idea for the
first act of our recital is that it takes place
under the sea in a magical kingdom that is
ruled by King Neptune, the king of the sea.
I need someone to be King Neptune and to
announce each number. And I want that
someone to be you. I've written down all
the words that I'd like you to learn and say,
and Mrs. Anderson and I have found a cute
song for you to sing. It's called 'What Kind
of a Noise Annoys an Oyster.'

"Mrs. Anderson will play it for you, and I
have the costume sketch to show you. Your
mom said it was okay with her. So, would
you like to be our King Neptune?"

Oh, boy, would I! I had seen a picture of King Neptune in a book, and he wore a crown and carried a thing called a trident, and he had an amazing long white beard that looked like ocean waves.

"Will I have a long beard?" I asked Miss Leah.

She and Mrs. Anderson laughed. "I don't think so, Tomie," Miss Leah said. "You'll be cuter without one. Would you like to do it?"

"Yes, Miss Leah," I answered. "Oh yes, yes."

Mom came in to pick me up. I told the great news. "I have a starring part. Hooray!"

"Isn't that great!" said Mom. "Your cousin Blackie would be very proud of you."

But I'll have a lot of work to do. The recital was going to be in three weeks on Saturday, May 23. Miss Leah said she would give me some extra rehearsals. Then she showed me the costume sketch. It was a green and silver short robe, called a "tunic," that had a flowing green cape with a silver border. There was a silver crown, a silver trident, and green shoes. It looked like something from the movies.

I can't wait to tell my best friend, Jeannie.

Chapter Three

Tuesday, May 5, 1942

Dear Diary,
 ~~Becaus~~ Because I am going
to be King Neptune, I have
to go to Dancing School for
some special practice.
 The first one is tomorrow
after school. I'll bring my
tap shoes to school with
me. Mom is going to let me
walk to Miss Leah's by myself.
 She'll meet me there.
 Y. B. F. I. T. W.

 Tomie

p.s.
 Mom told me that if I make
a mistake, I can just cross it
out, because this is practice and
Miss Gardner won't see it.

On Wednesday, after I had lunch at home, I tied the shoelaces of my shiny black patent leather tap shoes together the way Mom showed me. I carried them over my shoulder so all the kids in the school yard could see them.

On the way down King Street, Miss Kiniry, my first-grade teacher, saw me.

"Well, Tommy," she said, "are those your nice tap shoes?" (The teachers all called me T-O-M-M-Y, not T-O-M-I-E.)

"Yes, Miss Kiniry," I answered. "I've got an extra part in Miss Leah's dance recital and I'm going to a special rehearsal after school. I'm going to be KING NEPTUNE."

"Well, that's very exciting," Miss Kiniry said. "Are Carol Morrissey and Patty Clark going with you?"

"No," I said. "Just me. I have to recite

some things to introduce each number and then I get to sing a solo, so I need extra practice."

"Good luck," said Miss Kiniry. "I know you'll be very good."

As I turned into the school yard, I saw Buddy and some of the other sixth-grade boys talking together. The way they were talking and laughing and looking at me began to scare me.

All of a sudden, I was surrounded by the bigger boys and they started teasing me. One said, "La-de-doo—gonna dance for us?" Another boy said, "What are those shiny shoes for?"

Then the boys began shoving me around. "What are you, a sissy?"

I kept looking around to see if my brother would stick up for me and help me. But Buddy was just watching and smiling.

Then they grabbed my tap shoes and started playing catch with them. I tried and tried to grab them, but they threw them over my head.

"Those are my special tap shoes," I cried.
"Don't break them." But the more I yelled,
the more they teased me. I started to cry.
"Buddy, help me, please!" I shouted.

Buddy turned his back as if nothing was
going on. I looked around to see if there was
a teacher monitoring the play yard, but I
couldn't see one. What was I going to do?
I needed help.

All of a sudden, Carol Crane and a few of the older girls in fifth and sixth grade grabbed the tap shoes.

"You bullies, stop that!" Carol yelled.

"Yeah, leave Tomie's tap shoes alone," Anna Yara shouted.

"Pick on someone your own size, you big jerks," cried another girl.

"Baby!" yelled one of the boys. "Gotta have help from girls."

"Here, Tomie," said Carol, handing me my tap shoes. "Stay here with us until the bell rings to go in."

"What am I going to do after school?" I was crying even though I didn't want to; I was really scared. "I have to walk to Miss Leah's by myself. What if some of those boys follow me and beat me up?"

29

"I live on Hanover Street," said a sixth-grade girl I didn't know too well. "I'll walk you. Those boys won't dare bother us! You'll see. I'll meet you right in front after school."

I was so glad. But I still didn't understand why Buddy didn't help me.

• • •

During class, the school secretary, Miss Philomena, came in and said, "Tommy, Miss Burke would like to see you in her office."

What did I do now?

As we walked down to the principal's office, Miss Philomena said, "Don't worry, Tommy. You're not in any trouble."

I sat on the bench under the big clock and waited until Miss Burke came to the door of her office. "Please come in, Tommy," she said. "Have a seat." I got in the chair opposite her desk.

"I hear that there was some . . . trouble in the school yard. Is that right?" Miss Burke said.

I nodded.

"I was told that some of the older boys were teasing you and throwing your tap shoes around. Is that true?"

"Yes, ma'am," I answered.

"Well," Miss Burke continued, "we can't have that kind of behavior in the school yard. I am going to have a talk with ALL of the older boys, not just the ones who teased you. That way no one will try to 'get even with you.' Does that sound all right?"

"Yes, ma'am."

"Now, would you like me to call your mother to come and meet you after school so you can get to Dancing School without any trouble?"

"No, ma'am," I answered. "One of the sixth-grade girls is going to walk with me. She lives on the way."

"Good," Miss Burke said. "And, by the way, Tommy, I suggest that the next time you have to bring your tap shoes to school, you bring them in a paper bag or something. So they won't be so noticeable. You can go back to your class now."

• • •

After school, the girl—whose name was Lorraine—was waiting out front for me. The boys didn't bother us.

I told Lorraine about being King Neptune, and Carol and Patty and Billy, and the song I was going to sing. Lorraine was very nice.

I said good-bye to Lorraine at the train tracks and went on to the Hamrah Building and up to Miss Leah's.

She was waiting for me. There was a big chair in the middle of the dance studio facing the mirrors.

"Okay, Tomie. The show will start with you sitting in the chair, which will be decorated to look like a throne under the sea." She showed me a drawing of what the throne would look like. It would be draped with fishnets, starfish, shells, and make-believe seaweed. "The whole scene will be set and the curtain will open. You'll wait until the spotlight hits you, then I want you to stand, holding the trident in your left hand, come straight down front, and begin your piece. Have you had a chance to learn any of it? You can read it today if you want."

"I don't have to, Miss Leah. I've already memorized it," I told her.

"Wonderful!" she said. "Here's your prop trident." The prop trident wasn't the final one. It was made of heavy cardboard. The real one would be made of painted wood.

"Okay? Curtain. Spotlight."

I stood up and walked forward.

I began. "I am King Neptune, the king of the sea. Tonight is the night for a bit of revelry."

When I finished the first part, I backed up to the chair. "Wait," said Miss Leah. "I have an idea. Why don't you turn around so you can twirl your cape and walk back to the throne, turn, and sit."

I pretended I had a cape and tried it.

"That will be great," said Miss Leah with a big smile. "Now, one by one, you will introduce each dance number."

My favorite introduction was for "The Pearl in the Oyster Shell." It was going to be an acrobatic dance. I couldn't wait to see that one.

Then, for the finale of Act One, I would sing my solo, "What Kind of a Noise Annoys an Oyster." It was a very funny song. I rehearsed it with Mrs. Anderson a couple of times. I was very lucky because songs were easy for me to memorize.

As I was practicing, Mom came in with my baby sister, Maureen. When we had finished the rehearsal, Miss Leah said, "Floss, the material and pattern for Tomie's costume came today from New York." Miss Leah unwrapped dark green velvet for the tunic, silver cloth for the decoration, and beautiful pale green soft China silk for the cape. Also there was a pair of acrobatic shoes that would be painted green. My silver trident and crown would be the rest of my costume.

My dad would make the trident out of wood and my crown would be made out of buckram (whatever that is) and painted with silver paint.

I was so excited that I talked about the rehearsal with Mom all the way home on the bus.

But I still wished that Miss Leah would let me wear that long white beard.

35

Thursday, May 7, 1942

Dear Diary,

I think Buddy got his friends to tease me in the school yard yesterday.

He came over to my bed last night after the lights were out. He said he'd beat me up if I told Mom and Dad about his not helping me.

Then he called me a big sissy and twisted my arm. - hard.

He scares me.

Y.B.F.I.T.W.

Tomie

Chapter Four

Friday, May 8, 1942

Dear Diary,

In school today, Miss Gardner told us that a citywide art exhibit would be in our school for a week, starting Monday.

It is work done by the 3rd, 4th, 5th, and 6th graders from all the schools.

"King Street School is very lucky to be chosen," she said.

I can't wait to get into 3rd grade. I hope they have an exhibit next year, too.

Dancing School tomorrow!!!

Y. B. I. L. T. W.

Tomie

Today at Dancing School we rehearsed our "A Couple of Couples" dance number. The number starts out with Carol and me coming in from the right and Billy and Patty coming in from the left, doing a FOX-TROT box step. We meet in the middle and all sing the song "We're the Couple in the Castle" from the movie *Mr. Bug Goes to Town*. Then we do our tap routine.

Miss Leah actually clapped when we finished. We were so proud. "It's just like Fred Astaire and Ginger Rogers, only double," Mrs. Anderson said. But Carol and I want to be Judy and Mickey because they're younger.

Next Billy and I practiced our "Uncle Sam Gets Around" special, and then I practiced singing "What Kind of a Noise Annoys an Oyster" for my King Neptune part.

It was a really good dance class. It's a little sad to think that we only have two more weeks of classes before the recital. Then Dancing School will be over for the summer and won't begin again till fall. Miss Leah always goes to New York City for a few weeks to study and "catch up on all the new techniques and trends," she says.

Miss Leah's mother, Mrs. Grossman, measured my head for my King Neptune crown and then she gave each of us—and our mothers—our packs of tickets for the recital. Mom took thirty to sell. Mom and Dad know so many people and Mom is sure that lots of them will want to come. Miss Leah's recitals are famous for being really good. The newspaper even writes about it, and this year Miss Leah thinks it will be the best one yet!

Chapter Five

Saturday, May 9, 1942

Dear Diary,
    Uncle Charles has to go to the Army on Tuesday, May 12. Nana will get a flag with a blue star on it to hang in the window. We are going to have a party for him tomorrow.

Y. B. I. I. I. W.

Tomie

On Sunday afternoon there was a good-bye party for Uncle Charles at Tom and Nana's house in Wallingford. Lots of his friends were there. Everyone was trying not to be sad, especially Uncle Charles's girlfriend,

Viva, and his best friend, Mickey Lynch. We had two of my favorite things to eat: celery stuffed with cream cheese and Mount Tom sandwiches. Mount Tom is something Tom makes in the meat grinder in his store. He grinds up hunks of ham and pickles and mixes it with his favorite mayonnaise, Hellman's (Nana's favorite mayonnaise was Cains). Tom decided to call this sandwich spread Mount Tom after the place where his brother, Uncle Jack, has a cabin. Tom invented it for all the Downey family picnics that they had on Mount Tom.

Then, just like every Sunday, Tom and I listened to "The Shadow" and "One Man's Family" on the radio before we left for home. But then I thought, *It won't be like every Sunday anymore without Uncle Charles.*

I'm going to miss him. Uncle Charles is going to a place called Fort Devens in Massachusetts for his "Basic Training," which is when the soldiers learn how to fight in the war. I want Uncle Charles to stay in our country so he'll be safe. Not like Blackie.

I told Tom, "It won't be as much fun without Uncle Charles around. He always tells me jokes and goes with us to Foote's for ice cream when we come here."

"Don't you worry, Timothy, me bucko," Tom said. (Tom called me "Timothy, me bucko" as a nickname.) "I'll make sure you have a good time when you come to visit. Then we'll have a lot of stories to tell your uncle Charles when he comes home. I'm going to miss my boy, too."

It's hard to think that Tom, my grandfather, is Uncle Charles's FATHER, and not just Mom's.

"We'll just have to make do for the duration," said Tom.

"What's the duration, Tom?" I asked.

"It's the time that the war will last," he
answered. "Everything is changing so fast,
and we have to be brave."

I know I'm lucky to have such a special
grandfather and such a great family.

Chapter Six

I can't find my diary key. Without the key I can't open my diary and write in it. I put it and my skate key under my pillow last night when I had to take a bath. I looked and looked all over, under the bed, under my bedside table, everywhere. My skate key was still under my pillow, but not my diary key. I decided I'd better tell Mom.

"I'm sure it will show up," she said. "I'll keep my eyes open for it when I'm vacuuming. Now, get ready because you have to leave for school."

On the way to school, I told Jeannie. She keeps a diary, too. So she understands how important it is for me to find the key.

"Maybe you could write your diary in a notepad," Jeannie said. "But that might be dangerous. After all, the whole point of a diary is to write down your innermost secrets where no one else can read them. That's why diaries have little locks and keys."

"Well," I said, "I hope nothing too important happens until I find the key." I decided that I probably could remember stuff and then write it in the diary after I find the key and unlock it.

After we went into our classroom, Miss Gardner said, "Class, in a little while we will go down to the auditorium to see the art exhibit. The kindergarten and the first-graders are going first, then it will be our turn.

So, open your reading books and we'll have silent reading until it's time to go."

I was excited about seeing all the art from other kids in other schools. I already knew some of the good artists at our school because Mrs. Bowers, the art teacher who came to visit every once in a while, would put the best pictures up on the bulletin boards in the hallways.

Mrs. Bowers liked my artwork. She always picked out my pictures for the bulletin board outside our classroom. She knew I was going to be an artist when I grew up.

"All right, boys and girls," Miss Gardner said. "Line up by the door. As soon as Miss Fisher's room has gone down to the exhibition, we will be next."

I was standing in front of Jack Rule, who

was much taller than me and was one of my good friends in the class.

"We haven't been down to the auditorium and the basement since our last air-raid drill," I whispered to him. An air-raid drill was when we had to go to a safe place in case enemy bombers came.

"Tommy!" Miss Gardner warned. I kept quiet. We went down the stairs and there was Mrs. Bowers, ready to welcome us.

"Well, well, well," she said. "Miss Gardner's second grade. Welcome to our first citywide art exhibit. Now, take your time and look at all the wonderful pictures hanging on the walls. The names of the children who did them, their grade, and their school are on the little cards next to each picture. Enjoy yourselves. And feel free to talk to each other about the art."

Miss Gardner frowned. I think she would have liked it better if we were quiet.

We walked around and looked at all the pictures that were hanging on special walls 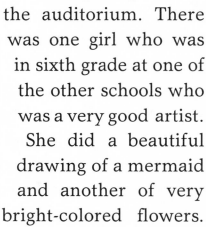that had been put up around the auditorium. There was one girl who was in sixth grade at one of the other schools who was a very good artist. She did a beautiful drawing of a mermaid and another of very bright-colored flowers. Her name was Jean.

After a while, Mrs. Bowers asked us to gather in the middle of the exhibition.

"Girls and boys, I'm asking all the students that come to see the exhibition to vote for their favorite picture," Mrs. Bowers said. "There are slips of paper and pencils on the table by the door. Please write down the name of the student whose picture you like best."

I wrote down the girl named Jean who did the mermaid picture.

The art exhibition was up all week. Buses brought other schools to see it. Some King Street students were asked to be "ushers" for the visiting kids. I was chosen by Mrs. Bowers because she knew that I loved art. The ushers had to meet the buses and show the kids the way to the exhibition. I did it three times. I made sure I pointed out the girl named Jean's pictures of the mermaid and the flowers.

"These are my favorites," I told them.

I also got to be an usher one day after school. Mom was there with some other ladies from the PTA to serve afternoon tea. I got to pass around a tray of cookies to the grown-ups who came to look at the exhibition.

The newspaper had photos and stories about it. There was a list of the favorite pictures for each grade. My favorite artist, Jean, was on the list.

The superintendent of schools, Mr. Brown, said, "The citywide art exhibition has been a great success. I want to congratulate Mrs. Bowers, the art supervisor, and all the students for such good work. And I want to thank the King Street School teachers and students for being such good hosts. I hope we can do this every year."

I hope so, too. I was already thinking of what I would draw for next year when I was in the third grade.

Chapter Seven

Tuesday morning, Mom, Buddy, Maureen and I went to Wallingford to say good-bye to Uncle Charles at the train station. It was very crowded with lots of people who were saying good-bye to the other young men who were going off to Fort Devens, Massachusetts, to learn to be soldiers. Uncle Charles was very popular in Wallingford, so he was put in charge of everyone going. Someone blew a whistle when it was time to leave.

"Okay, men," Uncle Charles shouted. "Say your farewells and get aboard." He hugged Buddy and me, kissed Mom and Maureen and Nana. He shook hands with his best friend, Mickey Lynch, and Tom. Then he hugged and kissed his girlfriend, Viva. He jumped on the train and it started up. It would go to New Haven and then to Boston, where a bus would take all the men to the Army camp.

Ladies were crying and waving handkerchiefs. The men were shouting and waving their arms, and then somebody started to sing "God Bless America." Everybody joined in. Viva was sniffling into her hankie. It was just like a movie.

Tom put his arm around my shoulders and said, "Don't forget, Timothy, we have to be brave."

"For the duration, right," I said.

"Right!" Tom said, smiling at me.

Chapter Eight

I still can't find my diary key. It's been five days since it's been lost and now I'm really worried. I hope I can remember everything that's happened!

I am getting more and more excited about next year when I'm in the third grade. It seems like all the really good stuff begins when you're in the third grade—the art exhibition and library time in school.

Every Friday morning a lady named Mrs. Cowing comes to King Street School. She's the Library Lady. Even though we didn't have library in second grade, I wanted her to know who I was, so I started to wait for her car to pull up. Then this Friday I

asked if I could help her carry in some of her
boxes of books.

"Well, aren't you a polite young man," she
said. "You certainly can help."

"I wish we could have library in second
grade, because I love books," I told her.

"Well, you don't have much longer to wait,"
Mrs. Cowing said.

I hoped that I could take out more than
one book a week from the school "library."
At the Curtis Memorial Public Library across
from the City Hall, the children's librarian
only lets us take out one book a week no

matter how many times we go. Mom takes us every week, but I'm usually finished with my book before I get home.

And besides that, the children's librarian has all the shelves marked with grade numbers, so if you're in second grade you can't take out any upper-grade books even if you're a very good reader like I am. Of course, I'm really lucky because we have lots of books at home, including tons of comic books that we used to get with Uncle Charles. Maybe Dad or Tom will keep doing that with Buddy and me. I hope so.

Jeannie comes to our house to read my comic books. Her parents are teachers and they don't think comic books are good things, so they won't buy her any. Every once in a while Jeannie just comes into our house and I'll hear her giggling in the living room. Especially when she's reading my *Little Lulu* comics.

Because I've been thinking about next school year a lot, I've begun to think about which third-grade teacher I hope I get. Of course, they never tell us whose room we will be in until we come back to school in September, but that doesn't stop me from thinking—and hoping. I hope I get Miss Bailey. She's very pretty, with blond hair and blue eyes, and she looks young like Miss Kiniry. And I noticed that she wears the color blue a lot, maybe to match her eyes. I'm sure she'll be a nice teacher. I smile at her every time I see her in the hallway.

Chapter Nine

The dress rehearsal for the dance recital was even better than I thought it would be. We got to see all the dance numbers and all the costumes for the whole recital. The show started with the "baby class." They went first every year because they were really little and Miss Leah didn't want to make them wait and wait for their turn. Everyone loved the baby class because they were so cute and so funny. They didn't do all their steps together, and last year during the recital one of the little girls turned around and saw her shadow from the spotlight on the backdrop. She never turned back around. She just looked at her shadow and bobbed up and down and swayed back and forth and waved at it. The audience laughed and laughed and clapped and clapped.

This year the baby class was going to be little fishes, and they sang the song about the "little fishies" in the brook who "swam and swam all over the dam." Their dance had a lot of wiggling in it. The audience would really love that.

"Under the Sea" was next. The music began and the curtain opened. I was sitting on my throne, wearing the crown and holding the trident. The other kids were sitting around the throne.

I wasn't wearing my costume, though, because Mom still had to finish it. But it would be ready for tonight. I stood up and came forward. Then, I began, "I am King Neptune, the king of the sea . . ."

One by one, I announced each act with a short poem that Miss Leah had written, until I got to the last one, which was "The Pearl in the Oyster Shell." That was the acrobatic number and the girl was very good. She did backflips and headstands— all sorts of tricks. Then it was time for me to sing "What Kind of a Noise Annoys an Oyster." The moms and the kids sitting out front laughed and laughed. And this was only the dress rehearsal! The first act was over.

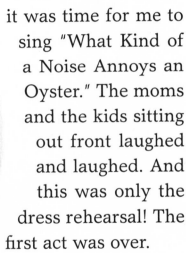

During the intermission Mom helped me change into a plaid shirt and blue dungarees for the "Uncle Sam Gets Around" number. Almost everyone was in it. It opened the second act.

Then Billy and I got into our "A Couple of Couples" costumes. We boys had on short white jackets with sparkly lapels, black pants, a silver sash called a cummerbund, and black bow ties.

Carol and Patty had on sparkly long dresses made out of this material that swirled when they turned around. Miss Leah, who was standing in front of the stage during the rehearsal, smiled and blew us a kiss when we finished.

The dress rehearsal went smoothly. It was going to be a wonderful show.

• • •

When we got home, Mom made me take a nap so I'd be "rested." After all, there was going to be a lot of excitement. Of course, I just lay there, wide-awake on my bed. Mom had pulled the window shades down, but I was too excited already.

When I went downstairs to have something to eat, Mom told me that Buddy wasn't coming to the recital because he was going to "Saturday Night Movies" with his friends at the YMCA. But Tom was coming! That was even better.

Then I tried my King Neptune costume on. It was wonderful, especially the green China-silk cape.

Suddenly the doorbell rang. "I'll get it," I yelled.

I ran to the door. I wanted to show off my great costume.

"Wait," Mom cried. "Tomie, wait."

As I was running by the coffee table, making my cape flutter behind me, I felt a tug at my shoulder and heard the sound of ripping. My cape had caught the edge of the coffee table and ripped along the silver border. I had ruined my costume! I started to cry.

Mom got the door. It was a neighbor wanting to know if we had any extra tickets for the recital.

Mom sent me into the kitchen while she talked to the neighbor. Then she came in to inspect the damage. "Well, it could have been worse," she said. "It only ripped along the edge. I'll sew it together by hand."

I stood there while Mom put the cape up on the ironing board to sew it.

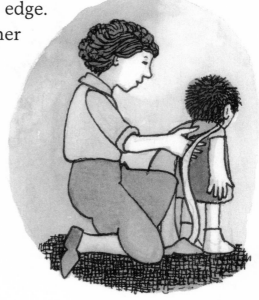

When she finished, she said, "No one will see it from a distance." She helped me out of the costume. I put on some shorts and a shirt. Mom had my other costumes and my best clothes for after the recital on hangers. And off we went.

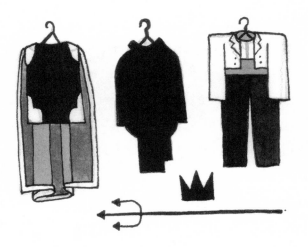

Chapter Ten

On the way to the recital, Mom gave me a pep talk in the car. "Don't think about anything but your lines and your song for King Neptune," she said. "The costume looks fine."

While the baby class was performing and the audience was laughing, we all got into our places for "Under the Sea." When the baby class left the stage, the curtain opened. The spotlight hit me and I stood up and walked straight down to the front of the stage. "I am King Neptune, the king of the sea. Tonight is my night for a bit of revelry!" I finished my poem, turned, and twirled my cape. I walked back to the throne and sat.

Then, one by one, I introduced each number until we got to "The Pearl in the Oyster Shell."

Now, my big moment. "What kind of a noise annoys an oyster," I sang, "when an oyster's in a stew?"

I don't want to brag, but the audience really loved King Neptune. There was so much applause. I was flabbergasted! I could see Dad and Tom standing up clapping.

The same was true of "Uncle Sam Gets Around." It was very patriotic. Billy Burns stood on one side of the stage and I was

on the other. Most of the Dancing School
students were in the middle. Billy and I
took turns reciting our parts. Then everyone
sang, "Uncle Sam gets around, but he don't
just drift. He's a-workin' and a-givin' everybody a lift." The audience cheered. "Don't
forget, we are at war," the song seemed to
say. "It's hard, but we WILL win!"

Everyone was doing a really good job
with their dance numbers. Finally, Carol
and Patty and Billy and I stepped out on
stage doing our fox-trot box step. We sang,
"We're the couple in the castle, way up

high in the air . . ." Then we did our tap
number. We were the stars of the recital!

When we came out into the auditorium
after the recital, all the chairs had been
moved aside so there could be dancing.
Miss Leah always did that!

I could tell that Dad and especially Tom were very, very proud of me and Carol, Patty, and Billy.

"I think Cousin Morton had better watch out," Tom said. (Morton Downey was our cousin and a famous Irish tenor who had a radio program.) "You might show him a thing or two."

Then Tom slipped a SILVER DOLLAR into my hand. "This is for a great job, Timothy, me bucko." Tom slipped a silver dollar into Carol's, Patty's, and Billy's hands, too. "Boy, Buddy doesn't know what he missed!" Tom said.

The small orchestra started to play and Carol and I did the fox-trot. Lots of people were dancing and having a good time. When the song was over, I went up to Miss Leah, who was wearing a long, beautiful gown.

"Miss Leah," I asked, "may I have the next dance?"

"Why, of course you can," Miss Leah said with a smile. So we danced all around the floor.

Soon it was time to go. We picked up Buddy at the Y and then went to Verdolini's for a pizza. Carol and her mom and dad were already there. We all squeezed into the biggest booth in the place and Carol and I ordered birch beer on tap, which was delicious. Dad said to the waitress, "We have some hungry performers here. We'd better have three large pies. A regular, a sausage, and one with the works."

You'd think that I would have fallen fast asleep when we got home, but I didn't. I could hear Buddy snoring over in his bed, but I was still too excited. I thought about King Neptune. I thought about oysters. I thought about Billy Burns and me and Uncle Sam, and I thought about our dance, "A Couple of Couples." Maybe I should be a dancing star instead of an artist, or maybe—just maybe—I could be both. Why not?

I wish I could write this all down in my diary.

Chapter Eleven

Every Sunday morning after the nine o'clock children's mass at St. Joseph's, the Sisters of Mercy had Sunday school for all the kids that didn't go to St. Joseph's Catholic School. We were getting ready to make our First Holy Communion. I was in the beginning class. We were studying the beginners' Baltimore Catechism and had to memorize certain prayers like the Our Father, the Hail Mary, the Glory Be to the Father, and most important, the Act of Contrition. That was a prayer you had to say when you went to confession.

None of us had ever been to confession.

Right before our First Communion we'd all make our First Confession. This was when you asked the priest to ask God to forgive all your sins. To do this, you have to go into a special place called the confessional.

It's like a big box with three sections. The Sister told us that the priest sits in the middle part and the people going to confession go in either side. She said that there is a little window that the priest opens (one side at a time) and then you tell him your sins.

You have to be very careful not to forget anything. Some of the Sunday school class are afraid that they'll do their First Confession wrong, because there is so much to memorize. I'm lucky I don't have to worry about that because I memorize things fast.

Next weekend is the Memorial Day holiday, so we won't have Sunday school on Sunday. We are going to have it on Friday after "regular" school. That's so funny— SUNDAY school on FRIDAY! We'll get to meet the kids from St. Joseph's School who will be making their First Communion, too.

Also on Friday we are going to have our Memorial Day assembly in King Street School. I will be in the Special Choir, which will sing the songs about the Army and Navy, Marines and Army Air Corps.

• • •

Before our rehearsal on Friday morning, Miss Mulligan, the fifth-grade teacher who plays the piano, asked me quietly if I would be all right. I told her that I thought I would be fine this time. And I was.

It was time for the assembly and our Special Choir sang our medley. Some of the other classes recited patriotic poems. One class did a Military Drill with cardboard rifles and a girl as the drum major twirling her baton.

Then Miss Burke, the principal, got up and spoke about the war. She said, "Boys and girls, I want you to know how important it is for us to tighten our belts *for the duration.*" She said we had to "support our troops" not only with "food and warm clothing, mittens and scarves, but with post-cards and letters." She spoke about Victory Stamps and Bonds that we would be able to buy next school year right in school. Then she ended her speech by saying, "We should all support President Franklin D. Roosevelt even if we don't agree with him." (I couldn't imagine ANYONE not agreeing with MY president.) All the teachers clapped.

• • •

We were let out early, so we Catholic kids went to St. Joseph's Church for Friday Sunday school. There were about twice as many kids there as usual. As the Sisters called our names, we formed two lines. "Look and remember who your partner is," the Sister said. Oh, boy. My partner was Jean Minor, my first girlfriend from first grade.

The Mercy Sisters seemed to be fussing over the St. Joseph kids more. "They know them better," whispered Jean.

We marched from the downstairs of the church across the street to the school, and into the front hall. We were divided into smaller groups and went into different classrooms.

The head Sister said, "This is where you will come on the Thursday morning of June fourth at seven A.M. We will then line up and have a procession over to the church for the First Communion mass. We will do a practice twice today and then again on Wednesday afternoon after school, when you will also make your First Confession." And she clicked a little clicker that she called a CRICKET.

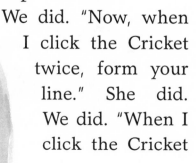

"When I click the Cricket once, stand up." She did. We did. "Now, when I click the Cricket twice, form your line." She did. We did. "When I click the Cricket again, go out into the hall and wait. Then I will click the Cricket for you to move in unison."

The Sister clicked that Cricket for everything: to march across the street, to march up the church steps, to march down the aisle, to stand, to kneel, to go up to the altar rail or to come back from the altar rail, to file out. It seemed to me that there were an awful lot of clicks.

We did it twice, like the Sister said we would.

Then, I walked down Linsley Avenue to catch the bus home.

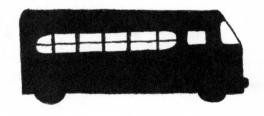

Chapter Twelve

The next day, we were up early to go down to the Bronx to visit my dad's sister, Aunt Kate, and her husband, Uncle Tony. My dad's brother Uncle Nick and his wife, Aunt Loretta, were going to meet us there, too. There was going to be a special Memorial Day mass for Blackie.

It was a long drive down to the Bronx and there were lots of cars on the road. This would be the last holiday before gas was rationed and we would not be able to get as much as we wanted, so a lot of people were traveling.

The Bronx was so different from Meriden. Above the streets were elevated tracks for

the subway, which came out of the ground
nearby and clattered on the tracks above your
head. It made the streets noisy and kind of
dark. There were always lots of people on the
streets. There were lots more stores and shops
than in Meriden, too. Many of the stores had
all the things they sold right out in front,
especially the fruit and vegetable stores.

Aunt Kate and Uncle Tony lived on Powell
Avenue in a big five-story building that
took up the whole block. In the center of
the building was a courtyard with a fountain and a garden. The garden had a sign
on it that read, "Home of the future Victory
Garden for the residents of this building."

I looked up from the courtyard and saw
a lot of flags with blue stars on them in the
windows. I didn't see Aunt Kate's. They

lived on the top floor, but I think their apartment looked out on the street instead of the courtyard.

We started climbing up the stairs—up, up, and up. There at the last landing was Uncle Tony waiting for us. My cousin Terry (whose real name was Theresa) was there, too. Aunt Kate was resting, so we had to be quiet.

Uncle Tony said, "Why don't you boys come up to the roof with me?" We climbed some more stairs. Uncle Tony opened a door, and there we were on the big roof of the apartment building. There were clotheslines with clothes and sheets flapping in the wind. People were sitting in deck chairs like they have at the beach, getting the sun. Uncle Tony showed us how we could walk all around the big square roof with the space in the middle

that looked down on the Victory Garden and the fountain—five floors down!

(I'm a little afraid of heights, so I hung on real tight to the wall before I looked down into the courtyard.)

When we got back downstairs, the grown-ups were all in the small living room. Aunt Clothilda and Uncle Mo and Cousin Frankie were there, too. They lived in the Bronx as well, not too far from Powell Avenue.

Terry took us kids, Buddy, Frankie, and me, into her small bedroom so the grown-ups could talk. (THAT never changes. They don't let us hear anything.) She turned on her radio and we listened to the singer she called her "HeartTHROB"— Frank Sinatra. Lots of girls liked him.

After a while Uncle Tony called, "Come out, kids. Dinner's ready."

The living room had a lot of tables put together. Uncle Nick, Aunt Loretta, and Cousin Helen had arrived. There were so many people, but frankly we were used to this on the Italian side of the family.

We kids sat at the far end, so (of course) I couldn't hear everything the grown-ups were saying. Aunt Kate kept crying very quietly. But I understood that. I wanted to cry, too. Because Blackie, Anthony, was my favorite cousin.

Just like at Nana Fall-River's house, we had food-food-food. Then the dinner was over. Suddenly, lots of sirens began to blow.

"Well, it's an air-raid drill," said Uncle Tony.

The grown-ups began to turn off all the lights and close the blackout curtains at the window.

"Hey," said Uncle Tony. "Why don't you boys come back up to the roof with me to see the searchlights."

"Sure!" we answered.

Buddy, Cousin Frankie, and I went with Uncle Tony to the roof. He had a small flashlight so we could find our way up the flight of stairs.

When we stepped out onto the roof, sirens were blaring all around. There were no lights anywhere. Bling, bling, bling. Suddenly, the sky was filled with searchlights moving back and forth. Oh, boy—this was exciting.

"This is only an air-raid drill," Uncle Tony said, "so they're just practicing. But if enemy planes did come here, the searchlights would find 'em and the anti-aircraft guns would shoot 'em down."

Then Uncle Tony got quiet. "Just like those Nazis did to Anthony's plane."

We just stood there—watching the searchlights, listening to the sirens.

"Well, this is how it's gonna be for the duration," Uncle Tony said, and we went back down to the apartment.

The grown-ups were sitting around the table, with candles burning, talking.

"Okay, boys," Mom said. "Time for bed."

Buddy and I were supposed to share the sofa.

"I'm not sleeping with him," Buddy said. "He stays awake and moves around all the time."

"Tomie can sleep in my bed with me," Cousin Terry said.

"Sissy," Buddy whispered in my ear.

• • •

I woke up early the next morning. I quietly crept into the living room so I wouldn't wake anybody. I looked at the window. There was Aunt Kate's Gold Star Mothers' flag. It was up so high that I wondered if anyone could see it.

*I guess the birds can
see it,* I thought, *or
maybe angels.*

After the Memorial
Day mass for Blackie,
we all went back to Aunt
Kate's and Uncle Tony's. It was real hard
on Aunt Kate. She sat in a chair in the small
living room, just looking at Blackie's photo-
graph and crying.

The long ride home was quiet. I guess we
were all thinking about Blackie. I was really
happy when we turned the corner of Fairmount Avenue. Somehow I felt good—and
safe—at home.

Chapter Thirteen

When I went to bed last night, my diary key was under my pillow. I didn't know how it got there, but I was really happy that it was found. I waited until I heard Buddy sleeping, then I took my diary and key and crept quietly down the hall to the bathroom. I shut the door and climbed up to turn on the light over the sink. I sat on the floor and unlocked my diary.

Someone had scribbled all over the pages and drawn bad pictures, too.

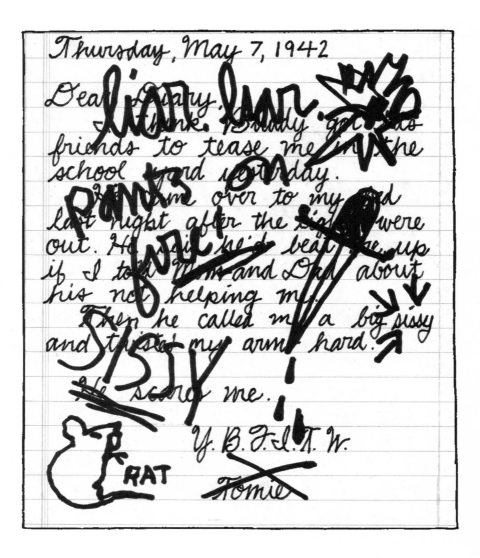

My diary was all spoiled! I closed it and locked it. I went back into the bedroom. Then I heard Buddy's voice whispering from across the dark room.

"If you tell, I'll get you."

It was then I decided to throw my diary away. I decided I'd never write in a diary again. I would REMEMBER everything I could. My thoughts would be safer in my head.

I answered Buddy with a whisper of my own.

"I won't tell—anybody." *Why is my brother so mean?* I wondered. I guess it's just like a war. I guess I'll have to put up with him for the duration.

• • •

My First Holy Communion wasn't like I thought it would be. All the boys wore white shirts, white ties, white shorts, white jackets, long white knee socks, and white shoes—everything white. The girls wore white dresses, socks, and shoes, and white veils like little brides. But the first thing that went wrong was that one girl fainted from not being able to eat (because you had to fast before your First Holy Communion). So all the partners changed and instead

of Jean Minor, my partner was a girl I
didn't know from St. Joseph's School named
Patty Tierney.

Then, when we were all kneeling at the
altar rail, a boy started yelling, "It's stuck in
my throat! I'm choking to death." A Sister
rushed up and whisked him away. There
was a bit of giggling from some of the kids—
and some of the grown-ups, too.

After the mass, we marched down the steps of the church over to St. Joseph's School, where long tables were set up so we could have breakfast. We had orange juice, milk, and doughnuts. Then Mom and Dad took me home because I had to change for school. So much for a special day!

On Sunday, though, when we went to church, I was able to go up to Communion with my family for the first time. That made me happy.

• • •

The last week of school turned out to be lots of fun. First of all, I won our final spelling bee.

At the School Dance assembly, our class did a minuet and Jean Minor was FINALLY my partner.

And—HURRAY!—I passed, so I'll definitely be in third grade next year.

• • •

Dad got his gas ration card today. He got a "C" because he works for the State

of Connecticut and needs to drive around for his job. There's a sticker with a "C" on it to put on the windshield, and a book of stamps. Every time he gets gas, he has to pay and give one of the stamps, too. "C" means that he can get more gas than "A's" and "B's."

Tom only got a "B" ration card for his delivery truck, so he can still deliver grocery orders mostly to the ladies who live in big houses near Choate School, which is a very fancy boys' school. He will be able to buy eight gallons a week.

Because Dancing School is over for the summer, I'll be able to go to Tom and Nana's store on Saturdays, as well as our usual Sunday visit.

Tom told me that when I visit on Sunday, he'll take me across the street to see Mr.

Andretti, an old Italian man, who has a big, big garden. He grows the best strawberries in Wallingford. They are just ripening, so we'll get some.

"Mr. Andretti is going to make his garden bigger and I'm going to buy his vegetables to sell in the store," Tom said. "We are going to call them Luigi's Victory Garden Vegetables. So, we'll both be doing our patriotic duty."

"For the duration?" I asked.

"For the duration," Tom said.

• • •

Everybody is talking about "the duration." We have to go to City Hall to pick up our ration books that we will need for meat, coffee, sugar, and butter. We will need to use our ration books "for the duration."

This coming Fourth of July, there will be no firework stands in Tracy "for the duration." The newspaper said that there will be a *final* Fourth of July City Fireworks display at Lewis Avenue Field, which means that we'll be able to see it from Fairmount Avenue. There won't be another one "for the duration." Even the movies have a message on the screen between films that reads, "This theater will soon be selling war stamps and war bonds to help our nation for the duration."

Air-raid drills, blackouts, rationing, shortages, no chewing gum, no fireworks, war stamps, war bonds, so many new things so fast.

And all *for the duration*.

The End

ABOUT GAS RATIONING

Gas rationing was all about rubber.

The military needed rubber for the tires on all of their vehicles, but the Japanese had captured the rubber plantations in the Dutch East Indies. These plantations produced ninety percent of America's raw rubber. President Roosevelt asked U.S. citizens to help by contributing scrap rubber so it could be recycled. Scrap rubber was "old tires, old garden hoses, rubber raincoats, rubber shoes and overshoes, and even bathing caps and hot water bottles."

The rationing of gas was voluntary at first. But not enough people cut down on driving, so by the spring of 1942, it became mandatory. It was hoped that reduced travel would help conserve tires especially.

To receive a gas ration book, you had to swear to the local ration board that you had *only* five tires (four on the car and one spare) and you needed gas. There were several categories.

About half of U.S. automobiles were issued an "A" sticker, which allowed four gallons a week. It was issued to people whose use of their cars was considered nonessential. When you went to the gas station, the attendant (no one pumped their own gas in those days) would make sure your mileage ration book had the same letter as the sticker on your windshield. Then you'd hand over your money and the coupons from your ration book and they would pump three or four gallons ONCE a week. No more! The "A" sticker was a white "A" on a black background.

The "B" sticker was a white "B" on a green background. "B" sticker holders were allowed eight gallons a week because the cars were deemed important to the war work.

"C" stickers were a white "C" on a red background. Of course, they were allowed even more gas a week. The "C" sticker and ration books were the most often counterfeited.

There were two more designations. "T," for truckers of all sorts, and "X," which were only given to Congressmen and -women in Washington.

The speed limit was dropped to forty-five miles an hour across the country. On the back of the ration stickers, the following was written in fairly large type so the driver would be constantly reminded:

To Save Tires
Drive Under 35

✔ **Share your car**

✔ **Check air pressure weekly**

✔ **Stop, start, turn slowly**

✔ **Cross-switch tires regularly**

Is This Trip
<u>Reall</u>y Necessary?

Gas rationing was extremely successful, and truly helped win the war.

Follow these links to find the lyrics of the songs mentioned in this book.

"Anchors Aweigh" (U.S. Navy)
http://www.navyband.navy.mil/anchorsaweigh.shtml

"The Caissons Go Rolling Along" (U.S. Army)
http://kids.niehs.nih.gov/lyrics/caisson.htm

"Marines' Hymn" (U.S. Marine Corps)
http://www.marinecorps.com/node/154

"The Air Force Song" (U.S. Air Force)
http://usinfo.state.gov/infousa/life/symbceleb/
airforce_song.html

"What Kind of Noise Annoys an Oyster?"
http://www.geocities.com/Area51/corridor/5109/
NovWKOyst.html

♡ DEPAOLA

Tomie dePaola has created over 200
books for children. His work has received the New-
bery Honor Award (*26 Fairmount Avenue*, 1999) and
a Caldecott Honor Award (*Strega Nona*, 1975). He
was also awarded the Smithson Medal, the Regina
Medal (from the Catholic Library Association), and
was designated a "living treasure" by the state of
New Hampshire. Most recently, he is the first au-
thor known primarily for children's book writing to
be honored with the Sarah Josepha Hale Award, in
recognition of a distinguished body of work in the
field of literature by a New Englander.

Tomie dePaola was born in Meriden, Connecticut, in 1934 to a family of Irish and Italian background. By the time he could hold a pencil, he knew
what his life's work would be.